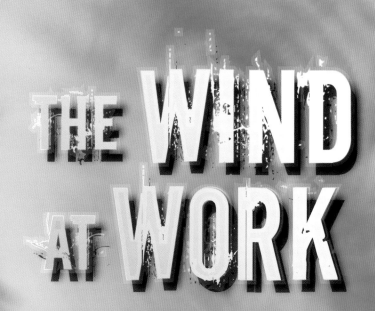

THE WIND AT WORK

Library of Congress Cataloging-in-Publication Data

Iwinski, Melissa.
  The Wind at work / by Melissa Iwinski.
      p. cm. -- (Shockwave)
  Includes index.
  ISBN-10: 0-531-17586-3 (lib. bdg.)
  ISBN-13: 978-0-531-17586-6 (lib. bdg.)
  ISBN-10: 0-531-18819-1 (pbk.)
  ISBN-13: 978-0-531-18819-4 (pbk.)

1. Wind power--Juvenile literature. I. Title. II. Series.

  TJ820.I95 2007
  621.4'5--dc22

2007012231

Published in 2008 by Children's Press, an imprint of Scholastic Inc.,
557 Broadway, New York, New York 10012
www.scholastic.com

08 09 10 11 12 13 14 15 16 17
10 9 8 7 6 5 4 3 2 1

Printed in China through Colorcraft Ltd., Hong Kong

Author: Melissa Iwinski
Educational Consultant: Ian Morrison
Editor: Lynette Evans
Designer: Steve Clarke
Photo Researcher: Jamshed Mistry

Photographs by: Getty Images (cover; windsurfing, pp. 8–9; yacht, p. 11; tornado,
pp. 20–21; pp. 24–25); **Jennifer and Brian Lupton** (teenagers, pp. 32–33); **NOAA:
The National Oceanic and Atmospheric Administration** (p. 13; waterspouts, p. 19;
tornado litter, p. 21); **Photodisc** (eye of storm, p. 22); **Photolibrary** (p. 7; p. 12; workers,
p. 29); **Stock.Xchng** (pp. 30–31, p. 34); **Tranz/Corbis** (p. 3; children, palms, pp. 10–11;
pp. 14–17; frogs, whirlwind, pp. 18–19; aerial photo of hurricane damage, monsoon,
pp. 22–23; pp. 26–27; Altamont Pass wind farm, pp. 28–29; Cape Wind Project,
pp. 32–33)

All illustrations and other photographs © Weldon Owen Education Inc.

THE WIND AT WORK

Melissa Iwinski

children's press®

An imprint of Scholastic Inc.

NEW YORK • TORONTO • LONDON • AUCKLAND • SYDNEY
MEXICO CITY • NEW DELHI • HONG KONG
DANBURY, CONNECTICUT

CHECK THESE OUT!

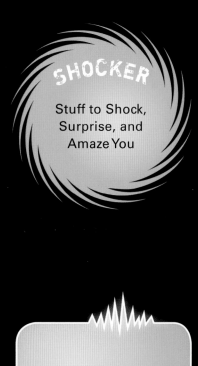

SHOCKER

Stuff to Shock,
Surprise, and
Amaze You

Quick Recaps
and Notable
Notes

Word Stunners
and Other Oddities

The Heads-Up
on Expert Reading

Links to More
Information

CONTENTS

anemometer (*an uh MOM i ter*) an instrument for measuring the speed of wind

circulation (*sur kyuh LAY shuhn*) the movement of air around the planet

funnel cloud a rotating cloud, also known as a tornado or a waterspout

prevailing winds steady, regular winds that blow over large areas of the earth's surface

turbine (*TUR biyn*) an engine that gets its energy from wind, steam, or water pushing on the blades of a wheel

windmill a machine with sails that are spun around by the force of the wind

· ·

For additional vocabulary, see Glossary on page 34.

In the word *anemometer*, "meter" means "to measure," and "anemo" is from the Greek "anemos" meaning wind. See if you can figure out what these words mean: *speedometer*, *pedometer*.

A tornado touching down

Wind is a powerful force on our planet. It can be a gentle breeze or an angry storm. You probably know that wind affects the weather. It affects the temperature of the air around us. It affects air and sea transportation too. Sometimes wind can cause a lot of trouble for people. It can destroy buildings and uproot large trees.

But do you know that wind can also help people? People have learned to **harness** the power of the wind to do work. Wind is the world's fastest-growing source of energy used to make electricity. Energy harnessed from wind powers machines. It also lights homes and businesses around the world.

What Is Wind?

Wind is air in motion. It is caused by the uneven heating of air and land by the sun.

1. Heat from the sun warms the land and air unevenly.

2. Warm air rises.

3. Cool air flows in to replace the warm air.

The process of cool air replacing warm air is called **circulation**.

9

Blowing Its Weight Around

Have you ever felt the rush of the wind on your face? Sometimes it feels strong enough to blow you over! But think about this: the wind is moving air, and air is almost weightless. Wind may not weigh much, but it can really blow its weight around!

On land, strong winds can smash buildings or push over large trees. At sea, strong winds can whip up giant waves. The waves crash into the shore and can flood the land. Strong winds at sea can also damage ships.

Long ago, sailors learned how to use the wind to move their ships. Back then, ships did not have motors. Instead they had sails to catch the wind. The wind would push the ships along. When the wind stopped blowing, the ships stopped going. Sailors had to either row or wait for the wind to blow again. Sailboats work in this way today.

That's interesting. The first sentence on page 8 is a question. It's as if the author is talking directly to me! I don't think she wants an answer. I just think she wants me to think about the question as I read these pages.

Wind can change weather. Warm weather may suddenly turn cool if a wind blows in from a cooler area. The wind can turn a sunny day into a stormy one. Dark clouds with rain and lightning may form where cool air meets warm air.

SHOCKER

People struck by lightning may survive. However, they will have burned, crispy skin where the lightning entered and exited the body. Their clothing and shoes may have been exploded off their body.

Weather affects everyone. Pilots and ships' captains need good weather to travel safely. Farmers watch the weather to know when to plant and harvest their crops.

People try to **forecast** the weather, but it sometimes does surprising things. For example, the wind really stirred things up in the United States during the 1930s. There was a drought in the Midwest. Large areas of farmland dried up. The fields turned into dust. Then strong winds started to blow. The lungs of anyone outside during the storms filled with soil and dust. The area became known as the Dust Bowl. Hundreds of families had to leave their homes and farms.

A farm in the Dust Bowl region, 1930s

It can be confusing knowing when to use *affect* and *effect*. *Affect* is usually a verb, and means "to have an influence on." *Effect* is usually a noun, and means "a result." The wind *affects* how we feel. The wind has an *effect* on how we feel.

13

A World of Winds

The wind may cause a sudden change in the weather. It may whip leaves around in a seemingly random way. However, the wind itself follows patterns. Some areas of the planet are windier than others. In some places, there are certain times of day when the wind often kicks up. In other places, there are certain seasons that regularly bring hurricane winds. Some places are more likely to have tornadoes than others.

Some winds occur over large parts of the globe. They are called **prevailing winds**. Other winds occur only in local areas. Winds are named according to the direction *from* which they blow. For example, a north wind blows from the north.

In the United States, there are several local wind systems. One is called a Santa Ana. This is a hot, dry, eastern wind. It blows toward southern California during the fall. Santa Ana winds often spread wildfires.

A Global Wind Pattern

Warm breezes are almost always blowing around the **equator**. These breezes are called trade winds. Trade winds blow steadily toward the equator from both the northeast and the southeast.

Northeast trade winds

Equator ▶

Southeast trade winds

A Local Wind Pattern

One kind of local wind pattern can be seen along a coastline. The wind moves in from above the water during the day. This is because land warms up faster than water. This means that the air over the land rises faster than the air over the water. However, at night, the wind travels toward the water. This is because land cools faster than water. The air over the water rises and is replaced by cooler air from over the land.

Warm air

Cool air

Winds of Change

Wind helps shape the land. It moves dirt, sand, and small rocks. This whirling dust chips away at the surfaces of other things. These things could be bigger rocks or mountains. Over time, pieces of these bigger things break off. The rocks or mountains start to look different. They slowly become smaller. This is **erosion** caused by the wind.

The heading and the first sentence are really useful. They help me predict what is going to be on the rest of this page.

Wind also blows the seeds off some plants. It moves them to different areas. Many seeds are well suited for being carried by wind. Some are shaped like fuzzy parachutes. Other seeds whirl in the wind like tiny helicopters.

Seeds often land and sprout in the crack of a rock. Even a small plant can make the crack bigger. This can break off a bigger piece of the rock and speed up erosion.

SHOCKER

The footprints that astronauts made on the moon will remain for millions of years. There is no wind on the moon to blow them away.

Whirlwinds and Waterspouts

Have you ever seen frogs falling from the sky? Have you ever felt fish slithering down your neck? People have told stories about frog storms and fish falls. There are even stories about bugs pouring down from clouds!

Scientists believe that the animals were carried into the air by whirlwinds and waterspouts. The animals fell to the ground when the winds died down.

Whirlwind, also called dust devil

SHOCKER

A strange thing happened in 1979. A heavy shower of frogs fell over a small village in Greece. The frogs covered the road so thickly that cars couldn't move!

Waterspout

Sometimes the wind spins and whirls madly. It picks up dust, sand, water, or even snow. It then twists it about. Strong, twisting winds over water can cause waterspouts to form. Waterspouts are narrow funnels of whirling air and water droplets. They reach high into the sky. Sometimes they suck up sea creatures, such as fish and jellyfish. Other times they suck up pond creatures, such as frogs and toads. The wind carries the animals far away. They later fall as very strange rain.

Tunnel of Funnel Terror

Tornadoes are the biggest, baddest whirlwinds of them all. Tornadoes can cause a lot of damage. Thunderstorms make the weather right for tornadoes to form. A **funnel cloud** is formed by the movement of the air. The fierce, swirling winds of most tornadoes move at between 70 and 320 miles per hour. Most tornadoes follow a path on land at a speed of about 30 miles per hour.

Did You Know?

A *tornado watch* means that there is a chance that a tornado will form. You should listen for sirens.

A *tornado warning* means that a tornado has been spotted. You must take cover right away. Head to the basement or to a bathroom or closet without windows.

Tornadoes sound like the roar of a waterfall or a screeching train. You might hear a high, ear-piercing whine.

Scientists use a special scale to describe the wind speed and the severity of a tornado. It is called the Enhanced Fujita Tornado Scale.

EF 0 This tornado causes damage only to trees and signs.

EF 1 This tornado can move cars and damage roofs and mobile homes.

EF 2 This tornado tears off the roofs of houses and uproots large trees.

EF 3 This tornado tears off the roofs and the walls of houses.

EF 4 This tornado levels houses and throws cars through the air.

EF 5 This tornado lifts homes off their foundations and carries them away. Steel buildings and structures are also damaged.

EF 6 This tornado causes such great damage that objects are no longer recognizable.

The word *tornado*, like the very strong wind it is, has itself been "twisted" around. It originally came from the Spanish word *tronada*, meaning "thunderstorm."

Powerful tornado winds drove this plastic record deep into a telephone pole!

Blown to Bits

A hurricane is another kind of extreme wind storm. Hurricanes begin over warm parts of the ocean. This is often near the equator. The ocean water warms the air above it, and swirling winds form. They can become stronger as the storm moves over the ocean. In some parts of the world, a hurricane is called a *typhoon*.

Did You Know?

Hurricanes in the Atlantic Ocean are given names of people! That way it is easier to talk about the storms when there are several brewing.

The eye of the storm is a part of the storm that is very calm. It is in the center. There is no wind in this part of the storm.

A hurricane forming

Monsoons are regular, seasonal winds. They bring large amounts of rain and lots of flooding. The strongest monsoons happen in Asia and Africa.

Heavy rain and wild winds are part of a hurricane. They cause the most damage just as the storm reaches land. Once it is over land, the hurricane begins to lose strength. This is because the warm water of the ocean is no longer feeding it.

Storm Chasers

Strong winds are part of some of the deadliest storms. We can learn a lot by studying the wind. Some people study storms as they are happening. They watch and listen for news of a monster storm. Then they race to where the storm is. These storm chasers follow hurricanes and tornadoes to learn more about them. They chase the storms in planes and cars. They risk being struck by lightning and hit with hail. They also risk being hit by the storm itself.

Storm chasers watch a category EF 4 tornado touch down.

Storm chasers might seem crazy, but they often gather valuable information. They use a tool called an **anemometer**. It measures the speed of the wind. They notify the National Weather Service about tornadoes that have touched down. People in the area are then warned by the piercing wail of tornado sirens. Storm chasers risk their lives to save the lives of others.

Now I get it! "Storm chasers" don't actually chase and capture storms. They search for and follow them. It's not like chasing someone in a game of tag. It is interesting that some words have slightly different meanings.

Catching the Wind

Wind does not always bring **destruction**. It can be a powerful force that people use to do work. People built the first **windmills** hundreds of years ago. Before then, most people had to grind their grain by hand. This was long, hard, tiring work. Their backs ached. Their arms became sore from crushing the grain with stones. Windmills harnessed the power of the wind. They put it to work. People no longer had to use their own energy.

Most windmills have a wheel of long blades that turn in the wind. The force of the wind turns the blades to create power.

Wind

Harmful:
- destroys buildings
- topples trees
- ruins crops

Helpful:
- helps boats sail
- creates electricity

Cutaway Diagram of a Wind Turbine

There is a generator inside the machine. It converts the spinning motion into electricity.

The blades are set at an angle. The angle can be changed to suit the wind speed or direction.

Generator

A tower holds the blades at a safe distance above the ground. There are electric cables inside the tower.

Today, people also use wind **turbines** to produce electricity. The use of windmills and wind turbines affects the lives of many people around the world. Maybe the lights in your school are using electricity produced by a wind turbine!

Farming the Wind

A wind farm is a group of wind turbines. Wind farms are usually found where there is a large expanse of open land. Places like this are found along coastlines and on high plains. These places are just right for wind farms. Wind turbines need a lot of space. They also need a lot of wind!

Did You Know?

Altamont Pass, California, has the largest wind farm in the world. It began in 1981. Altamont has 7,800 wind turbines. It makes electricity. It is also a place where experts study the use of wind energy. They develop and test improved turbine designs.

Wind farms produce electricity, but they are not problem-free. They can be very noisy. Sometimes birds such as eagles are injured or die when they fly into the turbine blades. People are concerned that wind farms are a danger to birds. However, studies have shown that very few birds die from **collisions** with wind turbines. More birds die from flying into natural objects!

Wind turbines are large, expensive machines. They seem to be worth the investment though. In the United States, wind farms produce enough electricity to power about 2.5 million homes.

Go With the Flow?

Will wind become the power source of the future? It is a good choice for several reasons. Wind is a **renewable energy** source. It does not cause pollution. It means people no longer have to depend on **fossil fuels** for electricity. Wind farms are also safer than nuclear power plants.

So why don't we build more wind farms? One reason is that wind farms are expensive to build. Also, much time and planning are needed before construction can begin. To find out whether a chosen area is a good location, experts must study the wind speed there for at least a year. A small difference in wind speed can make a big difference in the amount of electricity produced.

Did You Know?

A wind-power card is now available in some areas. It works in a similar way to a phone card. A wind-power card can be bought for about $15. It buys 750 kilowatt hours of wind power. This is enough power for an average home for one month.

Wind farms make clean, **efficient** energy. Many people believe that wind farms are a positive alternative to fossil fuels and nuclear energy. Wind farms do not give off any dangerous substances that harm the **environment**. Electricity from wind energy is also cheaper to produce.

However, some people worry that wind farms are dangerous to birds. Others complain that they are noisy, unattractive, and take up a lot of land.

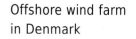

Offshore wind farm in Denmark

WHAT DO YOU THINK?

Do you think people should be building more wind farms to help meet increasing energy needs?

PRO

I think wind farms are a great idea. We need to do what we can to help the environment. We just need to select their locations wisely. This will decrease the risk to birds and reduce other bad effects.

Nantucket, Massachusetts, has an alternative to a land-based wind farm. The Cape Wind project is the United States' first offshore wind farm. The plan is to place 130 turbines several miles from land.

In Denmark, scientists studied offshore wind farms. They found that birds usually avoid turbines over the ocean. Placing wind farms offshore also removes other negative effects, such as their noise.

CON

Land is a valuable resource too. Wind farms use up so much land. They are also very noisy. Building offshore wind farms is a step in the right direction. However, we still need to find better ways to meet our energy needs.

GLOSSARY

collision a crash between two objects

debris (*duh BREE*) the remains of something
broken down, litter

destruction complete ruin

efficient (*uh FISH uhnt*) working well without wasting time or energy

environment the natural surroundings in a place, including the plants
and animals, landforms, bodies of water, and climate

equator an imaginary line around the middle of the earth,
halfway between the North and South poles

erosion the wearing away of land by water, ice, or wind

forecast (*FOHR kast*) a prediction of what will happen, especially
in regard to the weather

fossil fuel a fuel, such as coal, oil, or natural gas, that was formed
in the ground or under the ocean from plant or animal remains

harness to control something for use

renewable energy energy from sources that can never be
used up, such as wind, waves, and the sun

Destruction

FIND OUT MORE

BOOKS

Boskey, Madeline. *Natural Disasters: A Chapter Book*. Children's Press, 2003.

Bundey, Nikki. *Wind and the Earth*. Carolrhoda Books, 2001.

Challoner, Jack. *Hurricane & Tornado*. DK Children, 2004.

Ganeri, Anita. *Wind (Weather Around You)*. Hodder Wayland, 2004.

Peterson, Christine. *Wind Power*. Children's Press, 2004.

Strom, Laura Layton. *Racing on the Wind: Steve Fossett*. Scholastic Inc., 2008.

Walker, Nikki. *Generating Wind Power*. Crabtree Publishing Company, 2006.

WEB SITES

Go to the Web sites below to learn more about wind and weather.

www.windpower.org/en/kids

www.weatherwizkids.com/wind1.htm

www.wildwildweather.com/wind.htm

www.eia.doe.gov/kids/energyfacts/sources/renewable/wind.html

INDEX

ABOUT THE AUTHOR

Melissa Iwinski is a freelance editor and author who has enjoyed working on various nonfiction books for children. She hopes one day to publish a fiction story and become famous. When she is not writing, she loves to feel the wind on her face as she rides her bike down the bike trails near her home.